Yud's Child

by

Joanne Wehman Gull

Brick Cave Media
brickcavebooks.com

Yud's Child
Published by Brick Cave Books

Illustrations by
Interior Book Design and Layout by Brick Cave Books

ISBN-13: 978-1-938190-81-0

Cover art: "Yud's Child" by Dan Corporaal ©2022
Internal Illustrations by Dan Corporaal ©2022
Final Illustration by Joanne Gull ©2022

Printed in the United States of America

Brick Cave Media
brickcavebooks.com

DEDICATION
to the
Universal Sacred Spirit

and to

Joseph
cherished child of my heart
loving sojourner
to whom I can never say goodbye
without tears

"...and see [how] the body
and the soul
were engraved by YUD..."

Abulafia

"The child sitting
in the dust is Your
destined bride; her
play will be stilled
and deepened into Love."

R. Tagore

Yud's Child

by

Joanne Wehman Gull

Brick Cave Media
brickcavebooks.com

INTRODUCTION

This narrative emerged from listening. Many years ago I would hear the words, writing lines on scraps of paper or penning a brief continuing plot as it dictated itself. Eventually I heard words verse into a lovely story. The words and phrases were sparse with thought spaces in between. Every moment spent listening delighted and enchanted me. The words issued from a source real if unnamable. As the words aged over the years I heard them wanting another dimension. The letters wanted to be dressed in more than an alphabet; they finally revealed the way they wanted to be pictured. This is the story that wrote and illustrated itself with a little human help from a lover of words and a lover of art.

NOTE TO READER

On our journey through life we meet fellow travelers, different from each other as the legendary pilgrims traversing the Canterbury trail. As we intersect we may encounter one who opens our heart, another who steals purse or peace. Another may support or abuse. Are these companions other than our self or reflections of our own heart as we traverse both our internal and external journeys? This story may be a spiritual journey of one's own heart. This story may be a psychological mirror of the aspects of a human personality. Or it may be just a simple story that the Child in you enjoys as you meet a gentle doe, a wandering cat, a pleasure-loving pig, a transforming parrot, a protective cobra, and a lost child as they find pleasure and refuge in each other. Whatever it is for you, may it touch your heart.

Hebrew letters breathe. They hold our hands. They seek us out. Some dance, all hold secrets, all respect mystery. Each is a sacrament. One day YUD came to visit.

YUD

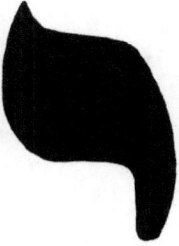

first letter of God's Name
  tenth letter of the Hebrew alphabet

primordial Atom
  Divine DNA
    single infinite point of flowing energy
pilgrim's progress
 myriad to oneness
   Thou to the human i
     silence of I AM and space song
whispered breath before God's spoken Name
     mystical invitation

  God's poem of one Word
  tear in the garment of time

Ruach hovering
  hidden spark of the Divine Spirit
      sigh of surrender
       ground of Being
     Love's teardrop

    Heartbeat
    Playmate
    Soulmate

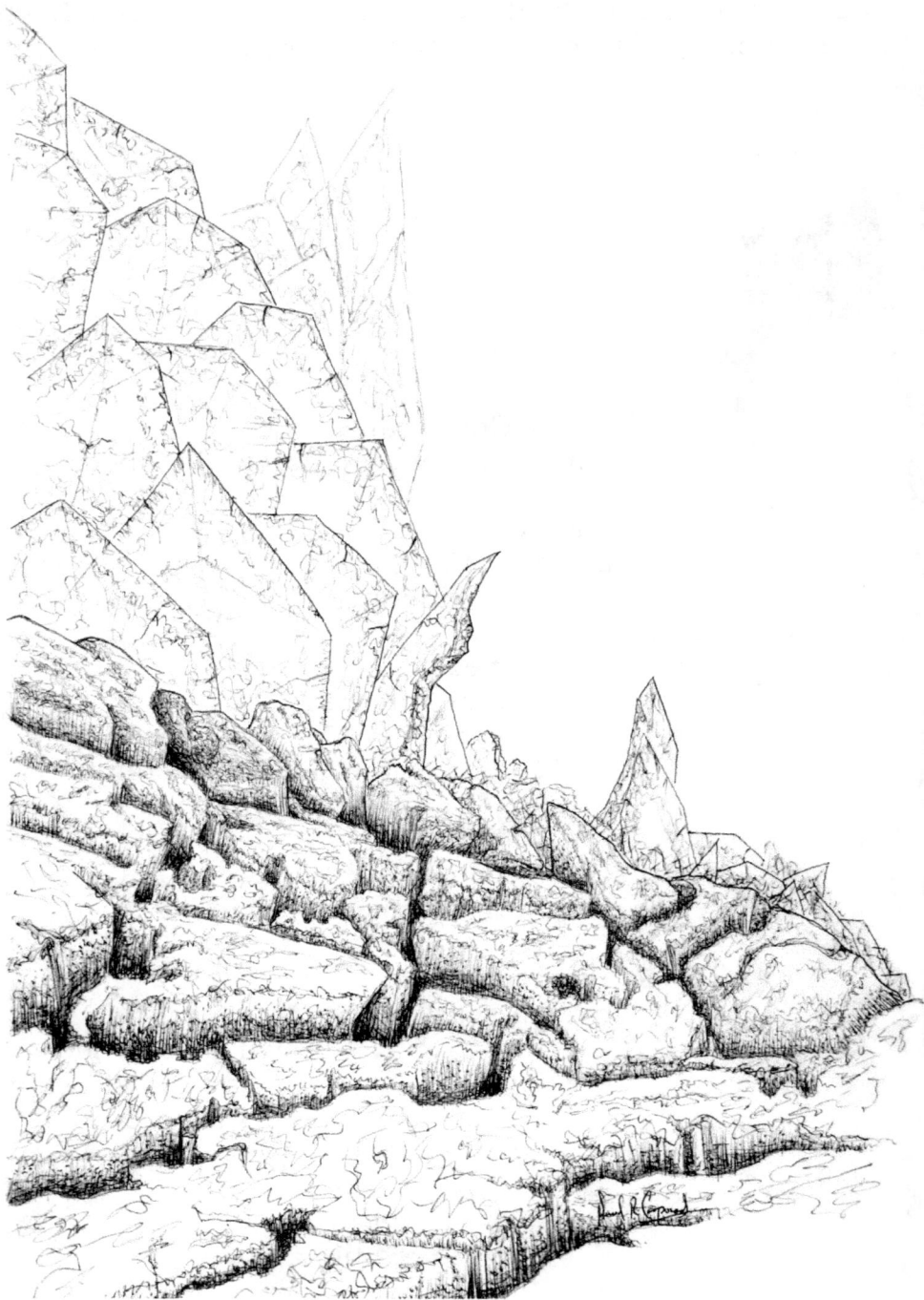

Shattered glass
A thousand pieces
Shards of stricken color
Sight of slivered ice

Upon the edges of a quiet lake.
Mountains stand above their space
And time is told by the way
The wheat bends in the fields.
Winter warmth is wound around
By currents from the oceanlake
Lapping on cave beach doors.
Spirit winds blow
Sometimes gentle
Sometimes not
And sometimes gales cross the cave
To bring all kinds of weather
To this no time springlike snowspace.

Baby doe
Caught limb cut to marrowbone
And bleeding by a trap set long ago
For game much bigger than herself.
So easily caught and brought to pain.

Hooded cobra slithers near to
Whisper that the pain is not so great.
The eye upon her hood says this is
G-d's eye and honest truth.
Pain is only just deserts
For such a fragile thing as doe.

Joanne Gull

In the shadows camouflaged
A quiet feline finds refreshment
Licking paws just pricked from
Playing cat and mouse,
Wishing that she'd had sense enough
To get a drink before the chase
And chafing that the mouse, too, got away.

She-cat awaits cobra's exit
So she can sit beside the
Baby Doe and tell her
How to die.

To die—
It's not so easy says
Strange Presence felt although unseen.
Doe hears and somehow knows that pain
Must need be healed and that it is
Ill of her to not acknowledge or help accept.

She-cat creeps to lock release
The bleeding paw
Somehow not unlike her own.
Together doe and cat lick broken pain
As doe learns how to self-heal all the hurt.

Then Lady-night sends quietness
To both curled up in timeless sleep.

But only for a moment.
Till awakened by the nightmare.
Nightmare! Screeching noise!
Lord Orddis comes to call
To spread deep terror, fear, and trembling.
Doe and she-cat now as one
With open eyes and prickling skin
Cling tight together.
Doe nibbles first her leg and then
The grass compulsively
While cat cleans clean on paw
Untouched by dirt,
Compulsive both in wake of Orddis here.
Little doe shivers as
Ice lightning sears the trees
Above their lair.
She crouches low
While she-cat sits aside and
Sheds a fearful tear.

Oh, the dark and running noise,
The black in black and fire fear,
The feltless pain of black despair.
There is no sheltered woods or good
But only Ordissness to fill the
Timespace of the nightmare now.
Even cobra closes door
To underground and trembles at
The presence of Lord Orddis.

Orddiswords scrape doe-cat's back
Until she feels oblivion.
Lord Orddis here. And dark.

Suddenly
Squawks Parrot,
"Here I am. Look at me."
"Here I am. Look at me."

Then tucks her head beneath ice winds.

Orddis here—remembered and renewed.
Bleak Orddis
Who can make doe and cat
Oblivious to being both apart or one together,
Or send calculating cobra underground.

Orddis,
Black broken glass
Of a troubled sea,
Jagged edges,
Imprisoned prism, impaled
Paralyzing pain,
Drawing blood from opened scars
Not even healed but only tended to
In days so long ago
With ointment and some cotton
Then left to fester till reopened now again.

There are no words to tell of Orddis.

 Parrot calls again,
 Urgent sounding
"Here I am. Look at me."
"Here I am. Look at me."

And tucks her head beneath ice winds.

Crying squeals to hurt the heart
From farmlands over hills
Come echoing on the icy winds.
Doe and she-cat huddled close together.
Little pigling scurries here and there.
Poor pigling with no hair,
Shivers pityingly from the icy winds.
She-cat stretches and mentally
Keeps doe-cat heat alive
While leaving lair to find poor crying pigling
Then leads it safely back to warmth
Between herself and doe.
Meanwhile cobra pulls her hood around
Her coiled scale-encrusted body
As her face and G-d's eye bow
In temporary submission
To the ground of Mother Earth.

Orddis rages on above.

Parrot sits stilled for just a moment.

Then
"Here I am. Here I am."
Coldest searing pain
Pierced by Parrot call of
Awakening life from slumberfear.

The echoes of the blackened glass of Orddis
Press in on she-cat and she cries.
Baby doe sleeps unaware
But rouses restlessly—but just a bit
While pigling recently rescued
Shivers slightly mid a dream
That promises perhaps
Some long, sought-for security.

Quiet.
Winds are gone
And softly stirs brave she-cat
In tired sleep.
Doe and pigling
Moved at she-cat's tears
Creep ever so close
To make protective bed
For her long-needed rest.
They lick her tears
And hold her close
So sleep can come
To heal and speak to her
Of promises that will be
Kept in days and nights ahead.

But now all three together stir
Aware that
Winds are gone
And even calling words are stilled
While Parrot sits alone above
With obscure thoughts.

The night's been dark and deep
And in their bones
They need to play.
With fear of danger unattended
They go above to race and romp
And chase each other
Thoughtlessly.

Snow has softened all the earth.
No sun, but warmth
From play and days remembered
Give a little space
In wounded hearts
That squeal and kick and run awild
Such footprints in the snow
As make designs to please
An Artist's eye and
Will be used to make
New snowflakes never
Born before.

Yet amid the play
Creeps deep concern
For cobra with her head
Pressed to Mother Earth.
Is it possible that
Even she would want to play?
And what would ease
Her calculating eye
So she could, too, be true
To better self?

Then suddenly they three recall
That foolishly not one had
Checked the door to underground.
What if Lord Orddis comes
And door is locked?
Their play is stilled
Beneath the tree
That homes brave honorable Parrot.
She senses these disturbing thoughts
In playful minds who
Should not play in fear.

"Here I am! Look to me!"
She speaks in dignity
And magically
Her words become
A handsome icy key.
Everyone who plays
In snow
Knows
That only icy keys made
From Parrot's words
Will open secret doors
To safety.

And so the cat and doe and pigling
Play some more
While Parrot guards
The magic key
And holds their fearful thoughts
For just a while.

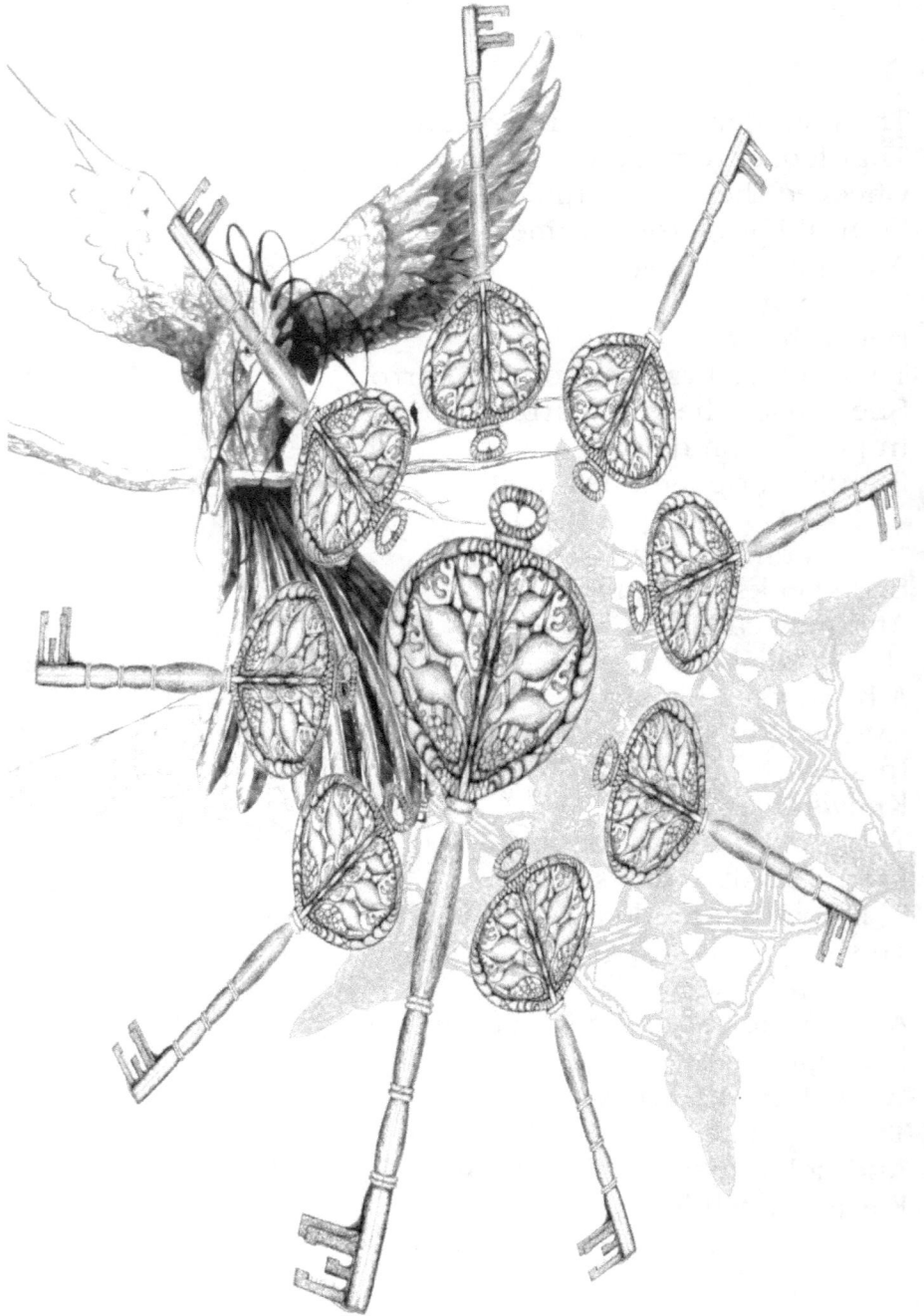

Very still in caverns deep below
Lay cobra with no play upon her mind.
Calculating cobra all alone
In labyrinth for fear of Orddis.
Not even surface quiet
Can touch her troubled heart.

While Pigling, doe, and she-cat rest
From mirthful play
Each feels a mysterious call
To find strange cobra.
But the journey to her lair
Is dangerous and deep
And only for the brave of heart.
Together, with no words, they
Start to dig beneath their havenhome
And find tunnels never dreamed before
Could even be on this fair Earth.
The first to weary is poor pigling
Who longs for play above the ground.
And doe, whose heart so wants
To do what's right
Just finds her lanky legs
Ill fit for this terrain.

But she-cat is untiring
As she finds one passage
Leading to another.
Her curiosity and set of mind
Find her deeper and deeper
Within the Earth—this cat
Who was made to chase frail mice
Above the ground intrepidly answers
Some little understood
Call within her heart.

Then all at once around a curve
She senses place secluded.
Comalike lies cobra
Who only breathes in fear and pain
Who knows nothing of the quiet
Snow so far above her home.
She-cat knows no word is spoken here.
She cannot talk or breathe too hard
Or dare to touch this cobra.
Nor can she think that it's her place
To even think that she can
Reach this cobra's heart.
This is cobra's home
And it is gift that
She is even so allowed
To enter into.
There is only presence
Of the two.

Suddenly
Inspired cobra, whose face
Has been so pressed to Mother Earth,
Arises
Slowly uncurls her body
Stretching muscles that far too long
Have lain in silent mystery
Majestic, commanding,
Oh so slowly that only
After timeless time
Is cobra now unfurled in
Stunning dignity.

Her glassy emerald gaze upon the cat
Begins to melt the sleep and hurt as
She-cat awakens bathed in ocean green.
They look upon each other.
She-cat holds deep
This tryst and
Knows that there is a sacred trust
Between them
Blessed by a greater Presence.

Cobra sees a restless hurt
In cat's submission.
It seems like endless ages
Since she-cat has shared
A space with doe and pigling.
It comes to her that maybe
She will not see again
Her beloved playfriends.
They are a part of her
But now they're gone
While she's begun a tryst with cobra
Which pulls her toward unknowns.

Cobra now has coiled herself
No longer rising up in either
Splendid dignity or imposition
But curls her length
In spiral beauty
Leading she-cat now to break a silence
With only just a thought
Directed toward the cobra.
"Why did you tell frail doe that pain
Was just deserts?"
Despite herself
The cobra's heart is touched.

But cobra's hearts are in
Their emerald eyes
And all her glance could answer was
That cobra is a cobra
And she a merely she-cat
And that nothing's wrong with that
Except the expectation
That it should be a different way.

And then she knows
That somehow she would soon
See doe and pigling
And that they too would find
Comfort in an emerald glance and
That there is a
Journey to be made
By all these different
In the light of One to come.

She-cat soon begins to feel
So faint for need of friends and
Familiar surroundings.
Cobra knows the cat will
Need some aid
So with no word
They two begin the journey
Upward
This time cobra leading
Through the labyrinths
To find the fastest most expedient way
To upward world.
Cobra's sense is true and swift
With she-cat following the
Emerald light which
Leads her way through tunnels
She had somewhat known but
Quickly had forgotten.
Cobra's strength and set of mind
Stand her well in this her world.
But weaker and weaker she-cat becomes
Till cobra has to let the cat
Hold tight upon her scaly back
And find an even shorter cut
For trembling she-cat's sake.

Ever so slowly green glazed light
Takes on a shade of sun
So long unfelt and so unseen.
When coming to this long-awaited space
She-cat's heart begins to beat
A rhythm heard by doe and pigling
Who run to meet their dearest friend.
They lick and kick—but not too much—
And carry tired feline back
To lair of sweetest hay in shadowed shelter
And even find a corner clean
For cunning cobra to curl up in.

Then all sleep in a somewhat peace
Being all together in one place.
A resting time is spent
In quiet space.
Pigling-doe listens to the
Cobra-cat's adventure tale
Understanding only
There was pain and ache involved
But cannot even begin to imagine
What is the meaning of that journey.
They are quite content to know
That knowing these two others
Is a privilege in itself.
For now it is enough.

In time in dreams they build a home
In which together they can dwell
And there are
Inner caves and outer caves.

Cobra likes the darkest corners
Pigling's place is everywhere
The tips of doe's ears are honey-touched
From feeding in the clover fields
And she-cat pounces the mousy shadows
Or mother scouts the homestead
Or basks in sun upon a breaker's home
To savor spray from ocean waves at play.
So in this dream come back to each
Memories of days of difficult play
A time when kicking play made
Snow designs
Remembered time
When fear of Orddis came to rest
When Parrot's words
Made icy key
To open secret door to safety.

But here there is no Orddis.
That's not so strange.
But where is Parrot friend
Who put their hearts at ease?
Not till now are they aware
Of how much missed
Is prismed Parrot.
Though resting in their new togetherness
They feel unrest for Parrot's absence.
Misty breezes blow at will
And not much play is in their hearts.
Timespace seems to lag a bit
And when they move
They go nowhere.
They're just together in a
Sort of now familiarity
Not yet aware of new amenities
That will hold a meaning beyond today.
So they are suspended
In unsuspecting sleep.

Awakening each together
A quiet sound is heard
Like the walking of a quiet flame
Or a snake molting skin.
Each senses new presence now.
As if one, each head lifts
From sleep
To see a shadow
Cast across the opening to their cave.
Soft sunflakes illuminate their home
Until their eyes become accustomed to
A shadow hovering, someone
Coming home to place he thought
Unknown to any but himself.
Before them stands
The hermit.

Earth brown wraps him round
Extension of the caves themselves
He wears.
With mountains carved upon his face,
Flaming rivers deep within his eyes
At once flowing ever, ever on
And then again direct, intense
Homed at where he looks
Rough his skin
But touch more gentle
Than the tongue of quiet doe
Lightning eyes that dim a cobra's
Emerald guile
Serene enough to lull the frets
Of pigling and she-cat.
Unadorned in true integrity
No sweetness or pretense—mere dignity
A woman's wisdom
A man's measure
Star upon a snowy mount
Feet that touch the earthly soil
Wrapped in solitude
And in his arms
His multi-colored heart
Sleeping Parrot now come home
Together wrapped in silence.

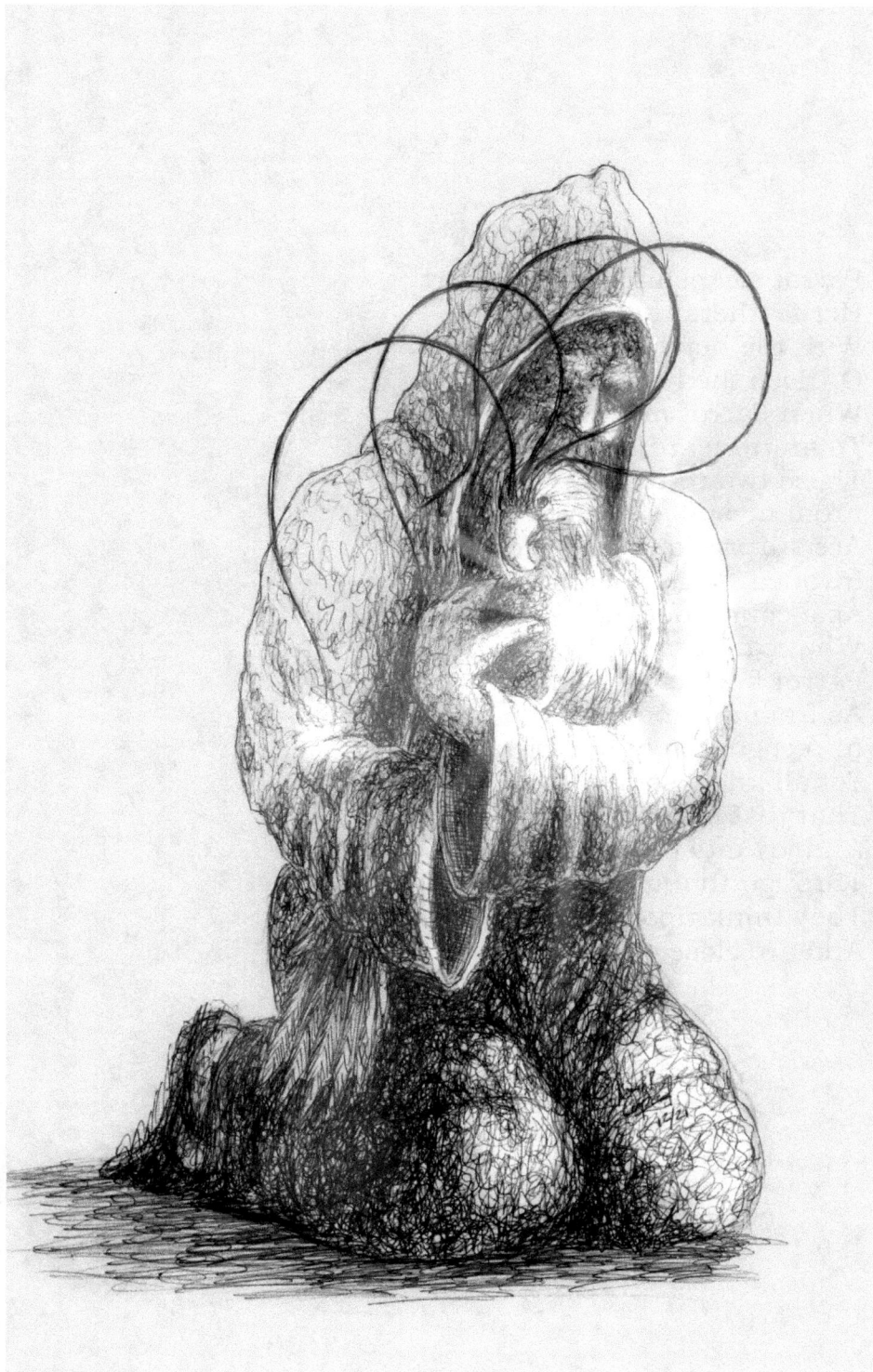

Parrot sleeps in hermit's heart
Her feathers rustling only
With the hermit's quiet breath
Or does the hermit breathe
When Parrot moves in rhythm
To an unheard song?
These two returned
From mystic journey
Are surprised to find their home
Invaded by such homely creatures
As a cobra, doe, cat, and pigling
What can it mean?
Parrot flutters wordlessly
As from a trance
In recognition of her friends
Yet all know somehow
That just for now their eagerness
And joy must be conveyed
Through thought alone.
They think upon each other
And are close.

Hermit hears within his colored heart
That this invasion of his hermitage
Is as it's meant to be.
His cave's been found
And made a home
For others so unlike himself.
But rumblings underground
Reveal to him that no place
Can be barred from one's real self
And so he sits and waits.
Strange hermit from the
Mystic mountain
Waits to hear
What should be done.

That no sound will be allowed
Seems known by some
Mysterious unheard message.
Cobra sits in darkest corner
While doe, cat, and pigling
Rest each as one.
Parrot blends in breath
And all become sensitive
To hermit sitting
Silent
And unmoving
One face turned down.
It is his other face
That fills the cave and their awareness
With somber rays of indigo
The hermit's other face of death.

For timeless space
They suspend themselves
One from the other
As though the universe and all beyond
Were hypnotized in
Total immobility.
Only pigling dares
To move upon occasion
But when not even her antics
Touch the hermit's consciousness
She settles down in unfamiliar discipline.
This breathing space
Is given
When all but life itself
Seems at a standstill
In death's presence.

Forever later it is given them
To move again—to waken
To this presence.
They're now aware
That they've come home
To someone else's house
And yet they know
It's home to them
And they must stay.
There's no apology
When one's in one's own home
Yet unfamiliarity keeps
Them quiet and in bounds.
Hermit stays unmoving
In questioning wisdom
Eyes cast down
As though his soul were elsewhere
And this cave were home
To just a body that needs shelter.

With thoughts of death
She-cat leaves the cave.
In death's shadow
She's been
Absorbed in darkness.

Staying still
Doe carries death within her heart
Enough to understand she-cat's need for space
To hold that pain.
Doe remembers cat's sweet comforts of the past
And heart-to-heart sends hope to she-cat's heart.

These two with death within their hearts
Measure life
In depth dimensions.
Now doe, the new befriender
And she-cat the newly comforted.

Again
Unable to be stilled
A moment longer
Little pigling wiggles next to
Quiet hermit
Wanting hermit's other face—
His eyes, his love.
Not consumed by death,
Pigling teases, plays the fool
So inappropriately
That hermit's heart takes
Pity.
Rolling on her back
And nudging hermit,
Poking nose beneath
The folds of brown
And smiling innocently
When she'd somehow gotten
Cragged face to turn
To softer streams and
Eyes to shine in silent laughing,
Pigling squeals in sheer delight.
Parrot's beak
Would then peek out
From Hermit's heart
As feathers flutter
Softly and relaxed.

Intently cobra lies
Against the wall
In shadows deep
Her eyes alive in muted green
For now.

Taking breath from active play
There is hardly any sound
When all become aware
Of ragged presence
At the entrance of their cave.
They stir in restlessness
And unfamiliarity
And even hermit
Who has never turned
His head for any other,
Turns to face the
Entranceway
While death retreats
Into hooded home.

There stands a ragged Child
Who's traveled far
From sometime, somewhere
So long ago.
Her hair is straggled
And her face is streaked.
She bears bruises
And her scars are deep.
She comes with nothing dear
But in her arms she holds
A comfort near—
A she-cat she has found.

She-cat has brought her home
Yet
Cobra knows her, too,
From that far away
Sometime, somewhere;
So much she knows that somehow
This is a cobra-child,
Child that has been guarded
In depths that only they have known
And once again
They know each other
And remember
Not knowing how, but
Just remember.

Without a word
The child comes to hermit's lap.
He holds her close
In folded warmth
His face of crags and streams
At peace in silent rocking.
She-cat lets herself
Be squeezed not unlike a doll.
She and cobra think
A lovenet round the child
Not unlike the arms
That hold her warm.

Joanne Gull

Doe and pigling unenlightened
Settle down
So child can sleep
While Parrot's colors
From the hermit's heart
Make stained glass eyes
Within the sleeping child.
She will see anew when she awakens.

A thousand pieces
Sea of colored glass
Managerie

She-cat held in Child's embrace
Recalls the cobra's labyrinth
From time she fought her way
Both in and out
To tryst with coiled companion.
Now too she knows that she's been
Where she is meant to be
But cramping from the lack of space
She longs for fields and water sprays
And maybe just a mouse or two
So wiggling free she jumps and runs
But in so doing
Wakes the sleeping Child.

Hermit and Parrot sleeping—breathe
While dreaming in another world.
So, blinded by the dark and frightened,
She-Child whimpers for some remembered comfort.
She slides from hermit's lap
Down to the floor.
Her comfort cat is gone
And so afraid this she-Child
Trembles cold and so alone.
She cries but through her tears
Sees cobra's eyes
Emerald deep and very still.
Some place deep within
She knows these eyes;
Once so long ago
They fed and clothed her.
This cobra once before
Had taken her to another cave
Deeper much than this
And breathed upon her
When she almost died.
This coiled presence
Lures her back
To corner darkness once again
Back and back to
Deepest recesses
She finds a place where she is sheltered
Where quiet breath is all that is alive.
Cobra coils in front of her
Like daring sentry
Protecting fragileness from being broken.
Both child and cobra
Look out into the cave

She-Child looking as it were
Through cobra's eyes.

But anyone looking into cobra's eyes
Would not see the Child
Or know that she was there.

As far as anyone can know
She has gone away again.

Timelessness...on and on and on...
Neither here nor there
No place, no space,
Nowhere.
Ice-not, stone-not,
Quiescence
Acquiescence to abeyance.
In a cave suspended
Like puppets left—not tended to
Except for she-cat, that is!
She was gone again, as usual,
And could not be a sentinel
This time.

All I's are closed.

Hermit's mind and heart
Are mountain high
In mystic mists
While death sleeps in his hood
With one eye open.

Parrot breathes
To keep them both alive
And that is work enough.

Pigling's daydreams slip
To childlike snores
Bonded cat and doe
Rest quietly in renewed affinity

While child and cobra
Coupled up in corner are
Shielded in green glow
From cobra's eyes
That somehow feeds them all
Just enough to stay alive.

Joanne Gull

This stillness—
Not unlike the quiet
Of the void when once
A Word was spoken long ago.
Not one word is heard
In this dark cave
For any sound would
Surely shatter green
And turn it all
To black abyss again.
If any sound were made,
Here,
Emptiness would only be;
For only special tones
Can resonate with green—
Mindful resonance
That does not betray the silence.

🕊 came so stealthily,
Gently stirring only sleeping air
Perceptible hardly
Even to Itself;
Except 🕊 has the gift
Of knowing Who it is.
🕊 has a mission,
Has been sent.
Of all the gifts, 🕊 is
The tenderest, the gentlest.
Incapable of harm,
Like vapor 🕊 touches the walls
To soften clefts
Closed in for length of time.

Then 🕊 circles Hermit-Death
And Parrot softly stirs.
Touch for Pigling is a blessing
Completely unperceived
But no less real.
Then circling softly
Above sick Doe,
🕊 dances to unheard music.
Here is where 🕊 has been sent.
This is where 🕊 is to home.
🕊 has not been told how,
But only knows
That neither 🕊 nor Doe could ever be
Until somehow
They made communion of themselves.

Slowly, Doe's fur stirs
Dulled from Death-so-near, so long.
Gently
י spheres around her trembling sleep
And brushes within her curves and folds
  י kisses her lashes wet with tears
And soothes the scars on crippled paws.
י takes away the Orddis fear
For י and Orddis are the black and white
That never can become a shade of gray.
So still is Doe as almost dead
Not knowing of a quiet life beginning.
י hovers Doe and holds her dear,
Then turns to face the eyes of green.

Those eyes—
They hadn't moved, but saw it all—
Steadfast, observant,
Cunning quiet, in reserve,
Waiting green of crystal—
These eyes that saw for two.
י knows this Cobra and her wiles.
י knows the Child behind the eyes.
And picking up velocity
י moves from Doe into the corner
Strong
To whirl around the shadowed pair.
Cobra knows the Child is safe.
She knows י as an echo from her heart
And lets herself be bent by י
Till round and round she curls
To form a circle doorway
Still within the cave;

A doorway that the Child could cross
And know her oneness still intact.
Wistfully, the Child arises
To stand on Cobra's body strong
Her feet upon a Cobra threshold
Holding hands on Cobra frame—
A Cobra halo round her body
Casting crystallining green
On walls and waiting hearts.

🔩 blew and danced—
Entranced the Child
Whose arms reached out
For precious gift.
She-Child saw in timely memory
A Cobra-Mother close, in dark.
She knows there'd been
A deeper chamber
To which she was forbidden
And now she knows
That she'd been watched
By 🔩 Who'd come revealed at last.
🔩 washes her, pouring swirls
Of Presence all around
While keeping Cobra in a treasured circle
As reward for all her care.
And holding sleeping Hermit-Death,
Completing Pigling's blessedness,
And drawing Cat back once more
Into the fold,
🔩 surged, resurged, and led the Child
To sleeping Doe.

Joanne Gull

Gently
She-Child stoops
To place the Doe within her arms.
She rocks fragility
To slow awkwardness.

To fall asleep alone
And then awake embraced
Is blessedness indeed.

The cave is different now.
Somehow
The current of ❧ Presence
Brings new strength
To each alone and all together.

Hermit-Death observes the Child
With fragile Doe embraced.

Parrot breathes ❧ Presence
Deeper than the others.

Pigling's heart leaps up to meet
The knowing glance of wander-Cat.

While Cobra
Melts to the floor
To circle all within a new door.

Then at once
In splendor green
All know their seeing
Is their being seen.

One can hold abeyance
Only for so long
Then the silence holds a thread
A cobweb design
That calls to travel on again
Call from some deep Presence

This call is heard
By Child first
She knows the Hermit's eyes
Would never be revealed
Till gift of flame
Came to the cave
By way of flame
Flame that led him
Through the dark
That warmed him in the snowy mists
And homed his shadow
Death within his hood
Since first she saw the Hermit's face
Turn toward her at the entranceway
When she'd been drawn to Cavehome
She had known that neither he
Nor any of them had been meant
To stay forever there
But Hermit's pain is deep
From this so long enclosure
His discipline so patient
While he sits within their center
Awaiting knowledge
Still they sit together
Held within green circle of Cobra's body
Child remembers now
The Hermit's warm embrace
And how she'd known
The quiet beating of
His Parrot heart so near to her

But even she had not been blessed
With eyes turned toward her own
She never really knew his face
She felt that something in him
Was far away and needed Life to touch him now

He had welcomed her into his house
And sheltered she-cat, pigling, cobra and the healing doe
He had encouraged she-cat's need to come and go
And pigling's inappropriateness had humored him
He'd been present for the healing doe
And allowed Cobra her shadowed secret corner
He'd accepted his position
In the center of the cave
And waited there in silence

Now Cobra knows from Child that it is time
To open green protective door
This she slowly does while shadows move
Across them all
To beckoned wakefulness

She-Child gathers leaves and twigs
Blown in from outer world
Cat hair comes from she-cat's mouth
For grooming was always her
Readiness for a journey
Pigling volunteers her horded leftovers
That no one ever knew about
And Parrot feathers are brought
From corners of the Hermit's robe
All are mixed with straw
From Cobra's corner lair
Then, tearing off a ragged hem
From her own dress
The Child piles all debris
Into a mound.

Joanne Gull

Hermit watches the preparations
And knows the time is near
He thinks
His waiting now is over
And Child's journey will be soon.

All sense Hermit's strength
Even Cobra is submissive
While not giving up
Who she rightfully is
The mound becomes an altar
Upon which they place their lives
Cobra shelters the light from emerald eyes
Until the cave becomes a midnight black

Slowly Hermit's eyes open wide
His lightning eyes
Dimming even more the Cobra's emerald guile
Lulling the frets of pigling and she-cat
Quieting the Child and doe
Awakening Parrot heart

All feel him now
Still wrapped in silence
They see the mountains and the cave walls
Carved ever deeper in his face
Flaming rivers from his eyes
Send fiery rays
To light the gifted pyre
The mound receives his blazing gaze
As does each heart
Hypnotized secure within this warmth
They see the mound glow deeper, deeper
Its embers indigoed against the waiting black
Hushed, they feel the quiet current
Of their awaited Guest

They knew this Presence
And were known
They remember
In the splendor green
That their seeing
Is their being seen

י who never went has come

Entranced
Surged and resurged
Then hovered close against them
They know it is again
A time of gift receiving
י breathes upon the fiery mound
Until the gift of flame fills the cave
In an endless moment's time
While all is shushed
The gentlest sparks of
Fire flame are placed as embers
Deep within the Hermit
All gasp at the precious gift received
Now it is given to them
To gaze into the Hermit's eyes
And he into their own
The gift of flame is his
To lead
And theirs
To follow
They were each alone
Together

But soon a nwe journey would begin.

For Child
Starting out has held
A certain fear, yet
Ignorance is eager
For the unexpected
She has slept
Waiting at the entrance
Of the cave—gathering strength
For a promised journey
A child is always ready to begin
She'd been told that Hermit was to lead
It wasn't for her
To tell him when to start
But Hermit's embered eyes
Fire a second thought

ﬠ holds him.

Hermit's journey once again is to sit still
To stay within his own cave
He could lead them all together
To the Mystic Mountain
But not now and
Never to where She-Child has to go
His eyes closed
His head bent low
His journey inward has begun
And once again
The face of Death fills the space
Death, the remembered, opens now his eyes
Where indigo promise had warmed the cave
Now black spreads molten in this chamber
Fear pulses through where recent peace
Had sung a soft sweet time

Child knows that nothing is forever
That everything is not
And nothing is
Her tears become a quiet hymn
Not unlike the music of the spheres
That plays among the constellations
Bringing them alive
Her tears flow
Between the parts of her becoming
Vantage points
Points that house the webbing threads
That soon will be the paths
To where she will be called
Her heart bids goodbye to
Doe and pigling, she-cat, and Parrot
Unsurprised, she welcomes
Cobra's opened eyes
Making doorway once again
She tightly wraps her arms
Around her Cobra's coil
And sees behind the Cobra nest
A guarded slit—the opening to the
Circuit way
Cobra looks to Child
With knowing glance of green
To courage breathe
Upon a frightened She-Child's heart
The others know they cannot go
It is the Child's journey
That must be walked

The darkness of remembering
Dark upon the dark – this new fear
The running noise, the black in black
And fire fear that sears and chars
Her tenderness
She'd been allowed to sleep the sleep
Of all forgetting
Had tasted deeper Presence
But now is called to waken to remember
A place within the labyrinthine caverns
Where forgetting and remembering
Face each other in silence
And sense the deeper Presence binding them

The shadows darkly taunt, tease, then
Play a kind of hide-and-seek with her
A tag and run
A blindman's bluff
And then again she is
The odd one out
In her shadowed memories
She recalls the days ago
When coming to the cave
Orddis's bird had eaten
All the scraps of bread
So all she had were crumbs
She knows the hunger once again
And sees the footprints with no maker
And the faces with no eyes
And hears the raucous calling terror that had sounded
In her heart and lured her on in dread
Had drowned the hymn within her heart

But she has Cobra now
And senses Presence deeper still
Together Cobra with Child proceed into
Another darkness
Obsidian caves, geometric planes
Dark upon dark
Like broken glass reflecting
One arched way within another
Never ending entrances to points
Dot-to-dot
Connecting cobwebs
Lines that lead
Deeper and deeper
Spiraled helix passages
Call now to Child
Cobra takes the lead
Knowing well the way of undergrounds
Cobra knows the hymn within Child's heart
Is growing brave

Gossamer threads cross her eyes
To reveal hag-shadows
Tormenting her with fear
Shadows hide along the walls
With specters from the folded caves
Jeering now at her

Spittle and a bruised point break her skin
And she begins to cry
Cobra's glare gives sight to Child
Pushing shadows back into the walls
Her tears fall upon a ghostly face
As it turns its back
She passes by
Along the way
Ghostly shadows jeer and she
Forgets she is a She-Child
Two ghosts turn their backs
And Cobra has to touch her eyes
To give her sight
One specter draws her close but falls across
A cliff to lie frozen broken while
She-Child hears distance dimmed
Souled music, shadowed promise
Of a beautiful symphony

They travel
Each cavern darker, more torturous than the one before
Convolutions crossing the years
Reflections mirrored only when Cobra turns
To cast green glance against obsidian blackness

It is not enough that she is in the bowels of earth
That there are caves that reach to nowhere
Now is the time for new depth
Now Cobra wraps
Around the Child
Together
They enter deep still waters
Of the river
Like a spiral
They together
Bore downward, downward
Beyond the depths
Of no place
Round and round
Deep and deeper
Together still
But Cobra knows the role of guide
Guide always one with her
But leading Child to the beyond

Together
Her feet
A vantage point
A point of turning
Her arms above her head
In awe and worship
Pointed fingers
Upward
Buoyed and weighted
The remembrance of an altar
Child now in submission
Unafraid

Joanne Gull

Currents flow in
Endless sound
Within obsidian walls
Now washed in water
Clearer than
The sea of glass

Now deeper Presence, ꜩ
Flows and rushes
Pushes currents
In and out
To enfold the Child
ꜩ centers the Child
To nowhere

Child and ℸ dance and flow
Move to silent sound
Child is washed
Tended
Unbended
The Mystic OM in symphony
Plays within her heart
Notes she had heard
Are now points of light and sound
Placed deep within her.

She stops to hear a tone
So clear—her heart hears
One note—it rings and echoes
On and on to awaken
The next—to blend in with the first
And once again, a tone to join
The other two
ℸ places deep within her
A chord of a thousand singing stars
A menagerie of harmony
Loves once given then removed
To live and play away from her
Are now singing echoes
That play within her heart.

ʬ

Indwells
Breathes
Sighs
Dances
Sings

Heartbeats
Playmates
Soulmates

SPIRIT SYMPHONY

ACKNOWLEDGEMENTS

If acknowledgment is the acceptance of something's existence, I primarily want to acknowledge Life. Life conditioned me to search and sojourn. How grateful I am to all the fellow travelers with whom I have been graced, especially my son, Joseph, Life's special gift to me. Over the years I have found Life's food and energy in the study of faith's myriad mystical traditions. Each tradition revealed Truth paths for me, but I am especially indebted to the teachings of Scholar-in-Residence Michael Shapiro in Scottsdale, AZ. I came to view the Hebrew letters as Truth tributaries: sacramental, symbolic, Spirit-filled. I want to express gratitude to Dan Corporaal for the beautiful art. He was painstaking in giving the text the pictures the words had patiently waited for. I also hold great regard for Sharon Skinner who found some merit in the text and risked publishing this book that defies genre. She has been patient and savvy, both admirable qualities in Life.

ABOUT THE AUTHOR

Joanne Gull was raised in Chicago, received her higher education and degrees in Ohio, dedicated her life to teaching, and boasts that her higher education was bested by all that her students taught her about life.

ABOUT THE ILLUSTRATOR

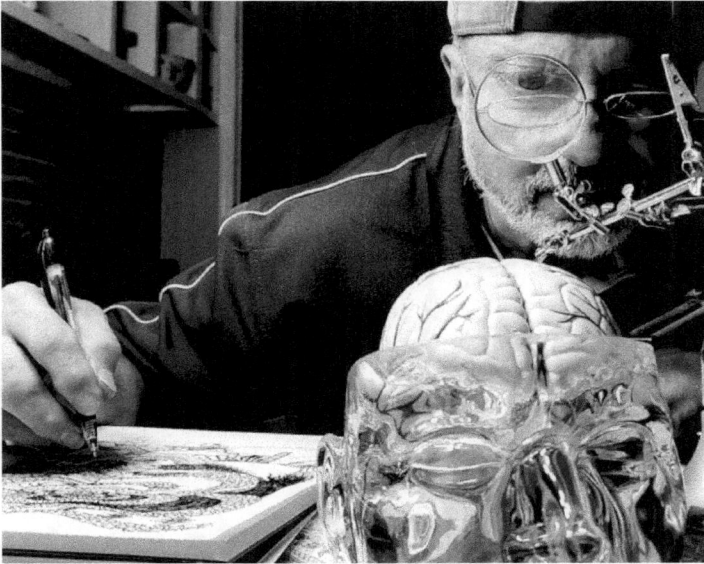

Dan Corporaal's illustrations for Joanne Gull's, Yud's Child, are influenced by his nearly 20 years of sketching in the Psychiatric Hospital where he was employed. Dan states, "The patients instilled in me a desire to translate their visions into reality." Find out more at: Danism.art